"I have never had a teacher. But every artist who has painted has been my teacher . . . and still is. I never went to an art school, though I was in one art class for a few sessions. I started by wanting to be a writer but quickly found the visual arts more natural to me. The desire to communicate has always been the strongest need of my life, and despite contemporary clichés to the contrary, I feel that art is a means of communication on the deepest possible level."

– RICHARD FLORSHEIM

"I have never had a teacher. But every artist who has painted has been my teacher . . . and still is. I never went to an art school, though I was in one art class for a few sessions. I started by wanting to be a writer but quickly found the visual arts more natural to me. The desire to communicate has always been the strongest need of my life, and despite contemporary studies to the contrary, I feel that art is a means of communication on the deepest possible level."

— Richard Florsheim

RICHARD FLORSHEIM

THE ARTIST
IN HIS TIME

THE BUTLER INSTITUTE OF AMERICAN ART
YOUNGSTOWN, OHIO

◆ Acknowledgements ◆

This exhibition and catalog are the product of many individuals and institutions, without whose help their creation would not have been possible. First and foremost, we wish to thank Dr. August L. Freundlich, Director of the Richard Florsheim Art Fund, for his initial idea of the exhibition and his careful stewardship of the project. We thank him also for his personal reminiscences of Richard Florsheim that he contributed to the catalog. None of this would have happened without him.

Domenic Iacono of the Syracuse University Art Collection and Neil Watson of the Norton Museum of Art in West Palm Beach have each submitted catalog essays whose scope and scholarship advance our understanding of Richard Florsheim, the artist and the man. We thank them for their skill and dedication. Dr. Iacono, one of the leading Florsheim scholars, was also instrumental in selecting the works that comprise this exhibition.

We are especially indebted to individual collectors and lending institutions who have so generously permitted us to borrow their works. They include the Syracuse University Art Collection, Syracuse, New York; The Richard Florsheim Art Fund, Tampa, Florida; William Meek and Harmon-Meek Gallery, Naples, Florida; Dr. August L. Freundlich, Lutz, Florida; Drs. Paul and Laura Mesaros, Steubenville, Ohio; and Mr. R.M. Pine, Elmhurst, Illinois.

We sincerely wish to thank the Board of Directors of the Richard Florsheim Art Fund for their generous support.

To those at the participating museums and galleries we extend our sincere gratitude –

At the Provincetown Art Association, Provincetown, Massachusetts: Director Robyn Watson.
At the Boca Raton Museum of Art, Boca Raton, Florida: Executive Director George S. Bolge, Curator of Exhibitions Courtney Curtiss, and Registrar Marc Ransdell.
At the Sordoni Art Gallery, Wilkes-Barre, Pennsylvania: Director Stanley I. Grand and Assistant Director Nancy L. Krueger.
At the Everson Museum of Art, Syracuse, New York: Director Sandra Trop and Senior Curator Thomas Piche, Jr.
At the Elmhurst Art Museum, Elmhurst, Illinois: Board member Robert M. Pine, Director Mary Moy Gregg, and Curator/Registrar Teresa Parker.
At University Galleries, Fisk University, Nashville, Tennessee: Director Kevin Grogan.

Jack Lemon and Landfall Press in Chicago deserve special mention for their unstinting efforts in the coordination of the artworks. Barbara Brown in particular is to be thanked for her indefatigable assistance as well as for having to put up with incessant phone calls from the editor. Her work could not have been more professional.

For photographic services, we wish to thank Arnold Newman, Norma Holt, Tom Van Eynde, Joe Rudinec, and Joe Traina of JA Studios. Elizabeth Seaburg in Chicago was responsible for all necessary framing of works for the show. We also thank Kay T. Morris of the Tampa Museum of Art for arranging transport of the Freundlich work.

Thanks always to Linda Jane Kurtz for her unwavering support and devotion.

> – Robert L. Kurtz
> Curator of Exhibitions
> The Butler Institute of American Art

Celebration, 1976, oil on canvas, 36 x 24 inches
Collection of Dr. and Mrs. August L. Freundlich, Lutz, Florida

◆ Preface ◆

The Butler Institute of American Art is pleased and indeed honored to present this traveling exhibition of the work of Richard A. Florsheim. Florsheim is a talent who for too long has been underappreciated, and it is our fervent hope that this exhibition will go a long way toward providing this wonderful artist the recognition which he so very much deserves.

It is altogether appropriate that the exhibition be entitled **Richard Florsheim: The Artist in His Time**, for seldom has an artist been so influenced by and reflective of his times than he. From the dark, haunting scenes depicting the ravages of the Second World War, to the colorful geometric modernism celebrating his beloved Chicago, to the calming, peaceful seascapes in and around Provincetown, Richard Florsheim's art encapsulates both the tragedy and the triumph of our times.

The Butler Institute of American Art has long been committed to showcasing distinguished contributions in the visual arts. We believe sincerely that in presenting **Richard Florsheim: The Artist in His Time**, The Butler Institute continues to satisfy its mission and to offer America a fresh look at a most significant artist.

While so many of the individuals associated with this exhibition are acknowledged elsewhere in this catalog, this entire project simply could not have taken place without the vision, encouragement, and support of Gus Freundlich, a friend not only of Richard Florsheim but of countless others in the arts across our nation. We thank him and the trustees of the Richard Florsheim Art Fund for their inspiration and for their generous assistance.

We also take the opportunity to reflect upon another side of Richard Florsheim, the side that recognized the importance of supporting artists who may no longer be in the spotlight but whose creative powers have not decreased. He cared very deeply about the forgotten artist–this exhibition both pays tribute and expresses gratitude to him.

> – Louis A. Zona
> Director,
> Butler Institute of American Art
> The Butler Institute of American Art

Earth Fire, 1970, oil on canvas, 18 x 24 inches
Collection of Drs. Paul and Laura Mesaros, Steubenville, Ohio

◆ Richard Florsheim, A Brief Reminiscence ◆

Beginning at some point in the late 50s Richard Florsheim was a casual acquaintance of mine. We met at some of the same art world gatherings, conferences or panels we both attended. When I became Dean of Syracuse University's Art School in 1969, (later Dean of the College of Visual and Performing Arts), I found that the University had over the years acquired groups of works by numerous artists or their studio estates and archives. In return the University had promised to preserve, display, and publish the art. Among the many artists were Federico Castellon, Richard Florsheim, James Earl Fraser, and Karl Schrag.

On their way from home in Chicago to their summer place in Provincetown, Richard and Helen Florsheim stopped in one day (probably 1972 or 1973) to see me at Syracuse. Our discussion soon turned to the University's promised publication, and at Richard's invitation I agreed to try the writing, which resulted in the book published by A.S. Barnes in 1976.

In the years that followed that first visit, we were together often in Chicago, Syracuse or Provincetown, and I came more and more to admire the man's artistic ability, his innate integrity and kindness to all. He had many friends, no enemies that I was aware of. He was a self taught artist, but had studied and knew all the masters. His studio was the neatest of any I had ever seen. Every tube and brush in its place, not a spot of color on the floor or wall, nor anywhere it had not deliberately been placed.

Florsheim is an old established family name in the Chicago area and one of comfortable means. Richard did not want people to think of his coming from wealth, but let it be known that he was a working artist, dependent on art for his income. At his frequent gallery openings he made sure that the refreshments at such affairs were never more elaborate than those of other artists. He never wanted any one to think he was buying his way as a rich man's son, but was fiercely proud of his independent achievements in art.

The purpose of the Fund established in his will did not surprise me and the several friends he invited to serve as trustees, ie: to assist older artists of past prominence with funds for exhibitions and museum purchases. The experience of being suddenly out of fashion hurt Florsheim deeply in his later years, so he empathised with fellow senior artists who went through the same experience.

It has been my privilege to share in the life and ideals of a good friend and artist.

– August L. Freundlich
November 21, 1996

©Arnold Newman

PHOTOGRAPHY BY
ARNOLD NEWMAN
1961

Night (Illuminations Portfolio), 1970, color lithograph, 13⁹/₁₆ x 18¹/₈ inches

◆ Illuminations and Metaphors ◆

The Graphic Art of Richard Florsheim

"Your environment comes in through your pores, through eyes, through all your senses and gets incorporated into a kind of general iconography, a kind of general storehouse or vocabulary of visual experience and visual information. Everything that I have experienced visually goes into that mill because I have trained myself through a lifetime of habit to remember. . . .I don't forget anything. It kind of enters into a tank and gets distilled and comes out as a distillation, a synthesis of experience. If I paint a city, it isn't a city it's all cities. If I paint the sea, it is all seas that I have experienced. . . .What I am looking for is not the particular but the universal."

– Richard Florsheim from an unpublished tape recorded interview, 1975

The years after World War II were stimulating; cities were changing and lifestyles were impacted by rapidly developing technologies. The 'jet' age had arrived. Speed, freedom, and soaring to great heights were positive characterizations of the new age and people became fascinated with the modern technology that was associated with the new age. Sophisticated advertising techniques and the continued growth of mass media industries, such as television and popular magazines, helped create a national appetite for a wide range of new products.

It was into this setting that Richard Florsheim found an audience for his prints. It was not a case of 'overnight' success, Florsheim had been making prints for twenty years. His accomplishments were not the result of mass marketing techniques or developments that made reproductions inexpensive and available in large numbers. Florsheim's success was merited because he made skillful images that synthesized elements of modern art and modern life.

Dr. August L. Freundlich in his 1976 monograph on Florsheim noted that the artist often sought to work out visual problems, especially those that were linked to the quality of light in a particular scene. This quality was recognized by the director of the Associated American Artists (AAA) gallery, Sylvan Cole, when he contracted Florsheim to make a print in 1959. The image was *Anchorage* [checklist 12] and it demonstrated Florsheim's ability to present a traditional scene in a fashionable manner. The artist used several visual devices

to make the image more engaging; the strong vertical accent of the masts had been equalized by the arrangement of the boats along the horizon. The tightly arranged hulls did not become too massive because Florsheim allowed light, brightest just above and behind the boats, to shine between the spars and the hulls. This light is reflected in the foreground water and extends the vertical lines of the masts below the horizon in the form of highlights. He also let the time of day remain ambiguous, allowing the viewer to resolve that particular issue. The setting for the print was Provincetown, Massachusetts, and the artist, never tiring of the possibilities that it offered him, would revisit this subject and the seaport many times in the next twenty years.

Florsheim developed a fascination for light, both natural and man-made. The ever changing light of day over Provincetown was always being affected by some natural phenomenon, such as storms out at sea, or weather fronts running quickly up the Atlantic coast pushed by the gulf stream, in addition to the daily changes caused by the angle of the sun in the sky. The artist spent many summers working in this resort town and was intrigued by the variations in light quality during the early, mid, and late summer. The interplay of light and shadow, and the optical adjustments he would need to make in his images provided Florsheim with a challenge. One method he used to focus the viewer's attention on the quality of light was to downplay detail and place the focal point of the image at a distance. Florsheim preferred working directly on a litho-

Lightning (*Illuminations Portfolio*), 1970, color lithograph, 13⁵/₈ x 18 inches

Morning, 1967, color lithograph, 23¹/₄ x 12³/₄ inches

Morning, 1967, lithograph, 23¹/₈ x 12⁵/₈ inches

graphic stone to achieve his desired effect. He felt that the image came alive when he worked without the benefit of a preparatory drawing because the design and stone placed demands upon his skill that needed to be addressed in an immediate and spontaneous manner. When he created his images of this seaport, Florsheim was reinterpreting a constantly changing scene that fascinated him endlessly and seemed to strike a chord with most collectors of his work and visitors to the Massachusetts resort town.

One of the artist's truly special talents was his ability to suggest variations of light in both color and monochromatic prints. The prints *Morning* [checklist 20 & 21] from 1967 are examples where Florsheim created black and white images that

were later reissued in color. In each print the artist has created an atmospheric effect by utilizing special characteristics of lithography, carefully controlling the amount of ink to create the impression, and in the case of the color print, choosing with care the ink that would best suggest the creative expression he was seeking. The prominent feature of these prints is the turbulent sky which was created in part by the solvent Florsheim used to spread his drawing ink on the lithographic stone. The chemical solution dissolved the greasy ink and helped disperse it over the stone, creating tide lines and areas of fragile ink formations that were deposited as the solvent evaporated. These formations seem almost organic.

His summers in Provincetown provided him with

Factory Fires (*Illuminations Portfolio*), 1970, color lithograph, 18 x 14 inches

ideas and inspirations that lasted beyond his stay. On his return to Chicago each fall, Florsheim would look upon the changes in the qualities of light in his Mid-western home town with renewed vigor, and before long his fascination would shift to the differences between natural and man-made light. Each type had its own special qualities and perhaps after a drive through an industrial area of Chicago, Florsheim would be inspired to investigate the atmospheric landscape of the city and its environs as they were impacted by the industrial plants and their emissions. He was not driven by a need to record the changes made to his native Chicago during a period of expansion or industrialization, rather he took advantage of changes in the light and recorded them in a way that was consistent with the manner contemporary people looked at the landscape. He discovered that the same lithographic treatment which helped define the natural turbulence of a summer sky also worked remarkably well for the urban sky. His palette expanded to include intense reds, oranges, and yellows; colors that were almost catalytic in nature.

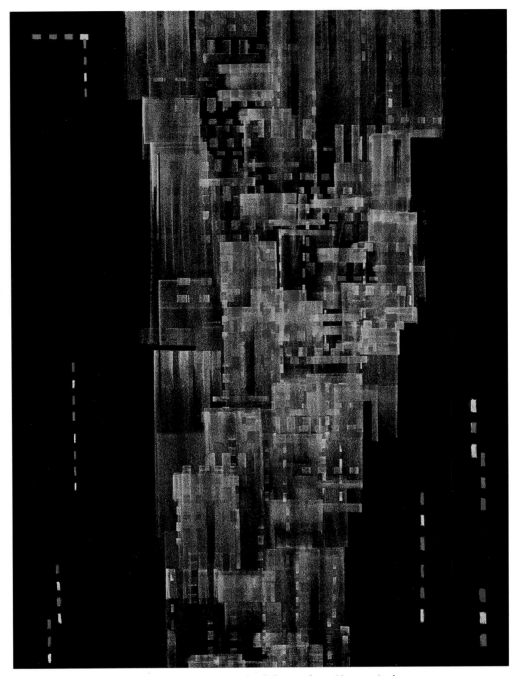

Neon Canyon (*Illuminations Portfolio*), 1970, color lithograph, 18¹/₁₆ x 14 inches

The portfolio *Illuminations* was issued in 1970 after four years of effort. Printed in Paris at Fernand Mourlot's lithographic workshop, the series of twelve prints represents years of investigation and labor to present the unique qualities of light that had intrigued Florsheim. The scenes he created for the portfolio were very similar to those which had been commercially successful for the artist and Associated American Artists Gallery. Their subject matter falls into three categories: seascapes and sailboats at anchor, urban night scenes, and industrial landscapes. The portfolio

also displays how Florsheim began to diversify his approach to structuring his compositions. When the scene was rendered in a vertical format the horizon line might appear low in the image, as in *Factory Fires*, [checklist 26] so as to emphasize the climbing streams of discharge from the industrial refineries. In *Neon Canyon* [checklist 33] Florsheim eliminates the horizon completely, while in the image *Night* [checklist 34] it has been raised above the mid point of the picture. The position of the horizon achieved several objectives among them focusing the viewer's attention on a specific area

Now Harbors Filled With Tangled Wreckage (War Portfolio),
1945, lithograph, 13^1/$_{16}$ x 8^{13}/$_{16}$ inches

of the image or balancing pictorial elements within the picture.

Illuminations was a series of images linked by Florsheim's interest in light and his ability to capture its unique role in affecting our perception of a scene. Earlier in his career, the artist made several portfolios or suites of prints that were associated by their subject. *Each Man in his Time* (1951), and the 35 prints that formed the *War Series* were attempts to work out issues that had troubled Florsheim since the late 1930s. The images dealt primarily with man's inhumanity towards his fellow man and the result of aggression on both a limited and global scale. The *War Series* was a six-year effort that began in 1940 before the artist entered military service and was completed after his return to the United States. Although the Series was produced in limited numbers, some images were printed in an edition of 10 while others 24, Florsheim thought the theme of the portfolio would resonate with a larger audience, especially those who had witnessed the horrors of war first hand.

In addition to using a common subject or theme to link the images within the portfolios, Florsheim often employed compositional patterns that were repeated from image to image. In order to concentrate the viewer's attention on a specific area he would construct the picture so that elements within the image pointed to, or were built up around, the focal point. Some images displayed an almost architectural construction as in *Now Harbors Filled with Tangled Wreckage.* [checklist 3] This kind of composition was important early in his career when Florsheim was creating images that had a psychological component and were exceedingly complex. He felt that a properly composed picture could aid the viewer by focusing their attention on key aspects of the image. The upward thrust of the tattered cruciform shapes of masts is countered by the tangled mass of line that brings the viewer's attention to the center of the composition. The dark, somber clouds in the background indicate that the smoldering ruins are recent and Florsheim skillfully worked them between the vertical structures as they recede into the distance. Later in his career

Neon Night, 1972, color lithograph, 22¹³/₁₆ x 17³/₈ inches

when the psychological aspects of his images were downplayed, Florsheim transformed these compositional devices to heighten the viewer's awareness of the new goals for his pictures.

In the mid 1950s the timing was perfect for Florsheim to begin a new approach to creating his art. Although it took many years for some people to forget the horrors of the war, many Americans turned their attention to new subjects. Florsheim was able to do the same; partly because he had sought professional help to cope with these personal issues, and also because he had for years expressed his feelings through his art. Themes of social oppression and suffering were gradually replaced by Florsheim's desire to explore other issues including the new 'jet' age and its impact on art. Abstraction, Abstract Expressionism, and the avant-garde movements of the post war period did not intrigue him, but the opportunity to create an art that evoked another sense of modernism seemed very exciting. In fact, Florsheim helped to establish a new visual vocabulary or style that seemed very modern to the typical American of the day. Marked by their angular and flattened architectural forms, or colors that seemed saturated with light, Florsheim's images were recognized as capturing the essence of 1950s design theory. He had developed his own iconography by mid decade: light that was reflected in water or clouds, urban scenes composed of "International Style" buildings, and complex cloud structures that seemed to be the result of pollution, were some of the most noticeable elements.

When the mid 1960s ushered in Pop art, the public became fascinated with images that actually used the newly developed technologies in their production process. Printed images that were closely linked with photographic technologies or that commented on the use of commercial art forms in contemporary image making quickly established a visual difference between 'old' and new. Florsheim's prints, with their 1950s constructions and iconography, became dated and associated with conservative tastes.

Florsheim understood the interest in the new art forms but felt his art depended upon the exploration of themes or visual problems that were personal and introspective. He, like so many other artists of his generation, rejected what they

saw as a slick, high tech approach to creating images. Occasionally adding elements that he found in contemporary imagery, Florsheim created several prints that incorporated stenciled text, billboard-style signage, or repetitious imagery as a major element. *Neon Night* [checklist 38] is an example of Florsheim's brief encounter with combining popular or mass media designs with his penchant for examining the effects of light and other compositional problems. These attempts were not all that successful and actually seemed more rooted in the experimental designs of the mid 1950s than the contemporary art of the late 1960s and early 1970s. Florsheim abandoned the effort to modernize his images and returned to the more comfortable surroundings of the seascape at Provincetown.

Florsheim once said that "One of the strains on my own personality was that I had a rigid dogmatic attitude. Well life isn't like that; it is a whole gradation of things in between." Throughout his career Florsheim remained committed to his vision of the role that art and artists play in life. Although many of his images investigate the impact of light on a scene, Florsheim was always aware that as an artist he was exploring man's sensitivity to his environment. When his subject matter was psychological he communicated on an emotional level that drew upon intuitions, his own and the viewer's, to help develop an understanding of one's self and deepen our appreciation of life. Like many artists, Florsheim drew upon his experiences to help create new images. Whether his work was commercially successful or not, Florsheim knew that it was only part of a larger whole and that his success as an artist would be judged not by individual images but by the totality of his career. In a brochure produced for his 1962 exhibition at Garelick's Gallery in Detroit, Florsheim said "I always seek the challenge of trying to make an ultimate statement, with the full realization that this is not possible." Perhaps the "ultimate statement" is not possible in a single image, or even throughout a career, but Richard Florsheim was an artist who consistently sought insights into that ultimate statement and shared his findings with any who cared to look.

– Domenic J. Iacono
Associate Director,
Syracuse University Art Collection

Cathedral, 1964, color lithograph, 17^9/$_{16}$ x 13^{15}/$_{16}$ inches

Cathedral, 1964, lithograph, 17⁹/₁₆ x 13¹⁵/₁₆ inches

Night City IV, 1970, wax & oil on board, 18 x 12 inches
Collection of R.M. Pine, Elmhurst, Illinois

Cathedral, 1964, color lithograph, $17^9/_{16}$ x $13^{15}/_{16}$ inches

"Lithography is my favorite print medium. As I am a painter with a pretty direct approach, the forthright orthographic quality of the lithograph appeals to me . . . l work directly, without preparatory drawings, believing that a lithograph, like a painting, must come alive as I work on it and must make demands on me which I try to meet. If I am sensitive to these demands, the living drawing tells me what I must do as I go along. For this reason, I prefer stone as a drawing surface, though I sometimes use zinc plates for color. *I always do my key drawing on stone.* There is no substitute for the responsive, flat, tempting, velvety surface of a good gray stone."

– Richard Florsheim

The Nature of Things:

The Paintings of Richard Florsheim

In this postmodern age, where irony is an artist's best weapon, Richard Florsheim's sincerity comes as a refreshing surprise. His paintings remind us that making marks is serious business; it links us from centuries past to centuries forward, hand to hand in the human chain.

Although Florsheim was born into an affluent Chicago family, he was no stranger to the hardships of an artist's life. His commitment to his work was tested, again and again. Perhaps the battles fought served to hone the desire down to its sharpest point, a clean bone of belief. Sometimes, the education of an artist has as much to do with what he or she is struggling against as struggling toward.

Thanks to the meticulous research and writings of Dr. August Freundlich, author of the 1976 monograph on Florsheim, much is known regarding Richard Florsheim's early development. We know that the decision to become an artist was bitterly opposed by a powerful father. Although he financed Florsheim's crucial years of study in Europe, he did so reluctantly, only after being shamed by his son's teacher, who promised, despite his limited means, to finance it himself.

Early on, Florsheim also had to battle charges of dilettantism. It is unfortunate for a serious artist to possess a family name that instantly calls to mind a chain of shoe stores. We know that Florsheim was sensitive to this, for when a critic mentioned the connection in an early review, Florsheim fired back a sizzling reply, angrily insisting that a distant family connection should have no bearing on his work.[1] He was right, of course, but the aura of inherited wealth behind such a surname persisted; it must have been a tedious battle to fight.

Florsheim's early promise is evident in the 1936 painting *Poles in Landscape* [checklist 43]. Executed in the difficult medium of egg tempera, it

Poles in Landscape, 1936, egg tempera on paper board, 14$\frac{1}{2}$ x 21$\frac{1}{4}$ inches

Men & Crosses, 1949, oil on stretched canvas, 14 x 15 inches

is an impressive accomplishment for a young man of twenty. Filled with references to a wide range of artists, it picks up cues from painters as far afield as the Mexican social realist Diego Rivera as well as the American heartland painters Grant Wood and Thomas Hart Benton. The staccato handling of the foreground and the vastness of the imposing sky is in perfect harmony with the vertical poles, which stand figure-like and foreboding, bringing to mind the dense and gothic paintings of Charles Burchfield. This painting is bursting with vitality as well as the promise of things to come.

Florsheim considered his pre-war years in Europe as seminal to his development. There, he studied art the way another student who was interested in numbers would study mathematics. He spent day after day examining his favorite works, carefully noting brushwork, coloration, chiaroscuro, and structure. When he returned to the United States, he would incorporate the elements that spoke to him most clearly in his own work.

But throughout his career, Florsheim's work would be most deeply influenced by the physical properties of what he looked at every day: time spent in Arizona and Mexico gives us the southwestern landscapes with their rich, earth-toned palette; the impact of the war years leads to the stark Kathe Kollwitz echoes in works such as *Men and Crosses* [checklist 49]; his identification with

Sajuaros, 1946, oil on gesso panel, 11 x 10 inches

the jumping modern city translates in his signature city paintings; summers on Cape Cod introduce him to the pictorial possibilities of sweeping sea and sky punctuated by bristling masts.

Florsheim might have dissected the European artists for structure and coloration, but it was the Mexican social realists Diego Rivera and David Siqueiros, as well as early American modernists such as Hartley and Dove, who most influenced the style and outward look of his early paintings and drawings. Florsheim's 1940 oil on panel *Sajuaros* [checklist 47], is a powerful homage to these influences, even while confidently staking out the artist's own territory. The paint handling, as well as the coloration, display a tip of the hat to Marsden Hartley. But the aggressive verticality and anthropomorphic characteristics of the cacti is pure Florsheim.

Cockfight, 1950, oil on stretched canvas, 24 x 32 inches

Another prime example of the powerful canvases from this era is *Cockfight* [checklist 51], a high key color interpretation of a barbaric event. This painting depicts the awfulness of the dueling birds with the vibrant bravado of the most beautiful still lifes. The cocks are locked in a dance to the death; a static group of villagers are characterized only by their sombreros, suggesting the blank, anonymous stare of onlookers to a practiced, primitive cruelty.

Mortal combat is an issue that concerned Florsheim beyond the graphic realism of his war-influenced work. The riveting *Monument to Monuments* [checklist 54], completed in 1954, displays distinct European echoes. This ambitious canvas bears strong atmospheric as well as structural parallels to the seminal works of Surrealist Giorgio

de Chirico. The vertical panorama is chock-full of visual information and movement. Numerous scenarios could be interpreted regarding the two battling monuments, but since this canvas was painted at the beginning of the Cold War, the most obvious interpretation would be the nuclear arm wrestling that was being waged between the United States and the Soviet Union. One of the few objects that Florsheim allowed in his studio was a fragment from the first exploded nuclear bomb[2], and the weight of a new level of devastation is evident in the titanic clash and bristling sky.

An overriding quality that emerges even in his early paintings is the sheer verticality of his subjects. This can be seen in his landscapes and

Monument to Monuments, 1954, oil on stretched canvas, 72 x 24 inches

Crucible, 1970s, oil on stretched/panel canvas, 30 x 40 inches

seascapes, as well as the figurative paintings. It is most distilled in the body of work that Florsheim is best known for, the city paintings.

When Florsheim painted the city, he treated it in the same way that he handled the human figures that populated his earlier works. If he painted his people as everyman, he treated his urban land-scapes as equally representative. The paintings are not site-specific urban portraits but rather paint-erly interpretations of the city as pure visual subject matter. Much like the urban abstractions of Piet Mondrian, where the city becomes a grid made up of geometry, poetry, and jive, these paintings never allow the viewer to forget that these are works about the act of living in, thinking about, and looking at the city.

Florsheim's city has a thin skin. The throb of the pulse is visible. Perhaps the influence of Chicago's International Style architecture, with that movement's love of glass, of structures made of planes and air, wherein Robert Hughes's phrase "even solid walls ought to look like mem-branes,"[3] informed Florsheim's unique perspec-tive. The artist's vision distills the city down to the essentials that the eye receives as impressions, rather than information: the flash of neon, the thrusting verticality of the skyscraper, the bounce of light against a sky thick with atmosphere. In Florsheim's hands, fenestration becomes a pattern of light, and modernity is seen as a blur of color and form.

Night City IV [checklist 56], gives little in the way of recognizable imagery, yet leaves no doubt as to the artist's intent for this canvas to be interpreted as a cityscape. The deliberate theatricality of the use of light and dark, the dramatic shimmer of reflected light as it dances across the water, all reinforce this idea. Florsheim has reached into his bag of painting tricks and pulled out the lessons learned in Italy years earlier when studying count-less Renaissance paintings. His brushwork has evolved into a more restrained and disciplined application of paint. The building up of pigment through the use of juicy brushstrokes has been replaced by a more thoughtful and analytical laying of paint-infused oil and wax mediums.

Florsheim continued with his urban themes into the 1970's with Crucible [checklist 58], but with an added twist. The painter has transferred much of

his inner anxiety regarding the unrest that was so prevalent in the inner cities to his canvases. Crucible is not a celebration of the city, but rather an unblinking glimpse into the B side of the modern urban experience. Here the building has become skeletal. The burning sky that surrounds it is thick and toxic. The city's shimmer has mutated into the rolling, engulfing smoke of nightmare.

Throughout his career, Richard Florsheim's life as an artist was marked by many style signposts. He has left us a rich legacy. In addition-to a consis-tent, varied, sometimes ravishing body of work, he bequeathed a helping hand through the Florsheim Foundation. He knew, better than most, that an artist's reputation, not to mention sales, can rise and fall according to a mercurial market; the integrity of the vision may not waver, but the bank account is another matter. The existence of the Foundation is a tribute to the man, who remembered, through his successes and his failures, that though an artist can spend hours contemplating the edge of a brushstroke, he or she may spend as much time contemplating the overdue electric bill.

This was a man whose love of beauty could not disguise a hefty dose of grit. The words he left behind are serious, thoughtful, tackling those capital-letter issues of Meaning and Beauty:

"I believe that we must communicate the order we find. It is essential that . . . in every language at our command, we tell each other the nature of things."[4]

In spending time with his paintings, through all their varied styles and subjects, this intent to get to the heart of the matter stirs us. Behind the brush, one senses a rabid, seeking, joyous curiosity and a simple faith in the endless possibilities of paint itself.

– Neil Watson
Curator of Exhibitions
Norton Museum of Art
West Palm Beach, Florida

Notes
l. August L. Freundlich, Richard Florsheim: The Artist and His Art (Cranbury, N.J.: A.S. Barnes and Co., 1976), p. 23.
2. Joan Hess Michel, "Richard Florsheim: Painter of City Lights," American Artist, vol. 24 (September, 1960), p.74.
3. Robert Hughes, The Shock of the New, (New York: Alfred A. Knopf Inc., 1980), p.191.
4. quoted in Michel, p. 75.

Luminescence (Illuminations Portfolio), 1970, color lithograph, $13^9/_{16}$ x $18^1/_8$ inches

"There are infinities of levels of communication. We can state the practical information which enables us to assemble or repair a piece of machinery. We can communicate abstract information through the device of mathematics. Art is the language for that area of emotional experience which cannot be communicated or satisfied in any other way.

In every case where a work of art has enduring value, it has something for which we cannot use words, a mysterious permanence of plastic meaning. This is the very quality of the object, the thing inherent in it.

I believe that the creative expression of man is essential to his well-being and harmony. The role of the artist is an essential one, for he gives form to our concepts. We must have this image of ourselves to have a sense of our being, on the deepest possible level of our conscious.

I believe, therefore, that we must seek the order that is around us with every sense, with every science and art at our command. We must communicate what we find of the ultimate truth and reality in every way that communication is possible. Then as individuals and as a people we will not fear the dark, but find it comforting and beautiful."

– Richard Florsheim

Buoy (Illuminations Portfolio), 1970, lithograph, 18¹/₄ x 14 inches

Spinning Machine, 1972, color lithograph, 12¹/₈ x 24 inches

Pines, 1954, color woodcut, 18¹¹/₁₆ x 22⁷/₈ inches

Blue Lights *(Illuminations Portfolio)*, 1970, color lithograph, 18 x 14 inches

Silhouette, 1979, color lithograph, 20 x 8 inches

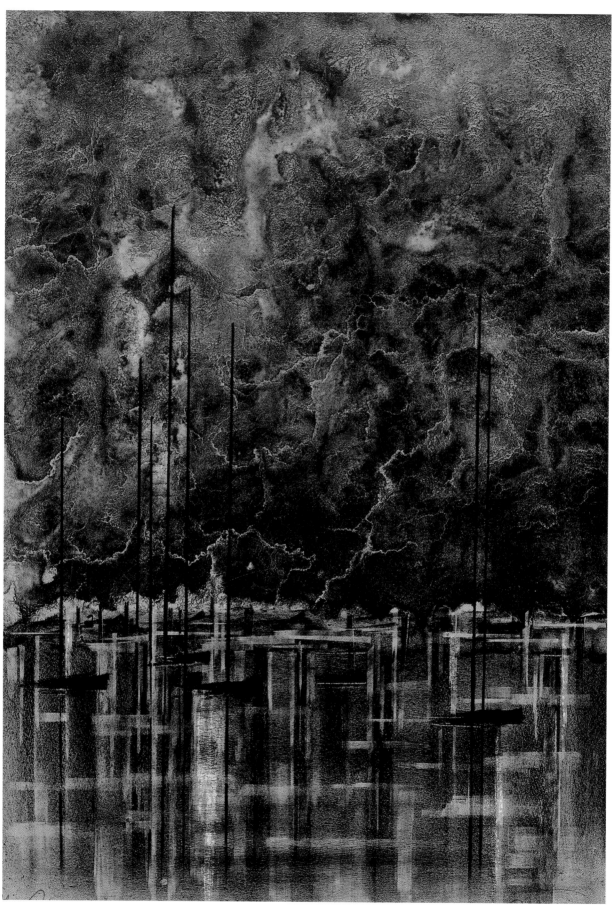

Mooring, 1970, color lithograph, 14 x 10$^{1}/_{16}$ inches

Mexican Walls, 1951, oil on stretched canvas, 36 x 20 inches

The Passage of Time, 1949-50, oil on canvas, 24 x 32 inches

Bridge Lights (*Illuminations Portfolio*), 1970, color lithograph, 18 x 14 inches

The Land Once More Regains Its Cycle (*War Series*), 1946, lithograph, $9^7/_{16}$ x $13^{11}/_{16}$ inches

14/21

R. G. Plastin

Inquisition, 1953, lithograph, 24^1/$_2$ x 16^3/$_4$ inches

Night Flight (*Illuminations Portfolio*), 1970, color lithograph, 13^1/$_2$ x 18^1/$_{16}$ inches

Crucifixion, 1953, lithograph, $26^{15}/_{16}$ x $17^3/_4$ inches

Attack, 1940, egg tempera on gesso board, 20 x 20 inches

Crowd, 1970, color lithograph, 15³/₄ x 22¹/₈ inches

Frontispiece

Fireworks, 1972, color lithograph, 29⁵/₁₆ x 18 inches

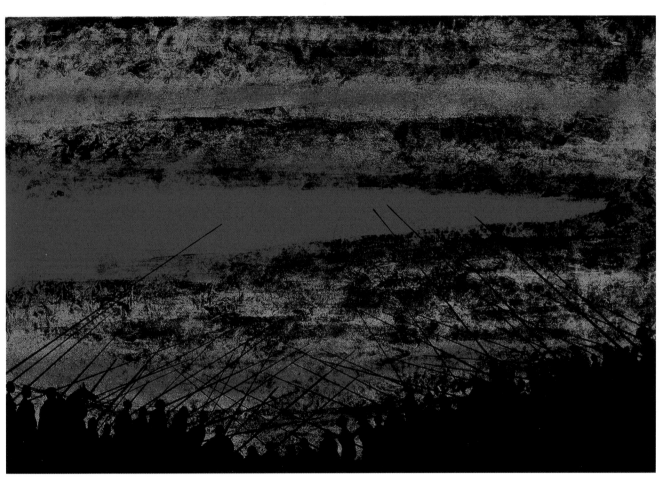

Combatants, 1969, color lithograph, 15³/₈ x 22³/₈ inches

9/10

R. 41

And Homeless Wandered (*War Portfolio*), 1941, lithograph, $9^{11}/_{16}$ x $12^{5}/_{16}$ inches

Pilings, 1954, color woodcut, 22³/₄ x 9⁵/₁₆ inches

Fire (Illuminations Portfolio), 1970, color lithograph, 13^1/$_2$ x 18^3/$_{16}$ inches

Cathedral, 1970s, oil on gesso panel, 36 x 12 inches

Refinery, 1961, lithograph, 13³/₄ x 9³/₄ inches

Dawn (*Illuminations Portfolio*), 1970, color lithograph, $13^9/_{16}$ x $18^1/_8$ inches

Variations on a Seashore, 1973, lithograph, 22$^7/_8$ x 15$^3/_4$ inches

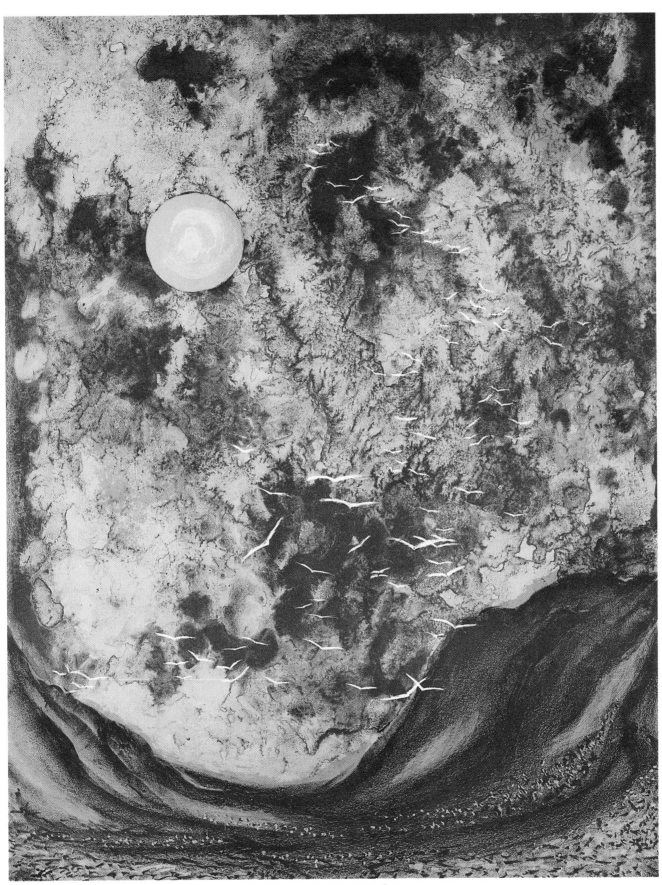

Sun and Dunes (*Illuminations Portfolio*), 1970, color lithograph, 18 x 14 inches

Insects (War Portfolio), 1946, lithograph, 5^1/$_8$ x 7^7/$_{16}$ inches

Skull, 1952, oil on stretched canvas, 40 x 30 inches

While Visions Weighed Him, Crushed and Speechless (*War Portfolio*), 1940, lithograph, 10^7/$_{16}$ x 6^1/$_8$ inches

Skyscrapers, 1962, color lithograph, 29$^1/_2$ x 10$^3/_8$ inches

Shoreline, 1962, lithograph, 9⁷/₈ x 13⁷/₈ inches

Richard Florsheim

Selected Solo Exhibitions

1935 Breckenridge Galleries, Chicago

1939 Quest Galleries, Chicago

1940 Quest Galleries, Chicago

1944 New School for Social Research, NYC

1946 The Art Institute of Chicago

1947 The Milwaukee Art Institute

1948 Luyber Galleries, NYC
Chicago Public Library
Beloit College, Beloit, WI
The Seven Stairs, Chicago
North Shore Art League, Winnetka, IL

1950 Leonard Linn, Inc., Winnetka, IL
University of Chicago
University of Nebraska, Lincoln
Esquire Theater, Chicago

1951 Elizabeth Nelson Galleries, Chicago

1952 Mandel Brothers, Chicago
Instituto Nacional de Bellas Artes,
  Mexico City, Mexico

1953 The Contemporaries, NYC
Galerie Gerald Cramer, Geneva Switzerland

1954 Landau Galleries, Los Angeles

1955 Jacques Seligmann Galleries, NYC
Philadelphia Art Alliance

1956 American Galleries, Milwaukee, WI

1957 Jacques Seligmann Galleries, NYC
Ohio State University, Columbus

1958 The Art Institute of Chicago

1959 Babcock Galleries, NYC

1960 Garelick's Gallery, Detroit
Associated American Artists, NYC
Oehlschlaeger Galleries, Chicago

1961 Shore Studio Galleries, Boston
Babcock Galleries, NYC
University of Wisconsin, Madison

1962 University of Maine

1963 Associated American Artists, NYC
Oehlschlaeger Galleries, Chicago

1964 Atlanta (GA) Art Association
Gallery 100, Princeton, NJ
Babcock Galleries, NYC

1965 Richelle Gallery, St. Louis
Flair House Galleries, Cincinnati

1966 Gallery of Modern Art, Scottsdale, AZ
Associated American Artists, NYC
Birmingham (AL) Museum of Art

1967 Cape East Gallery, Provincetown, MA

1968 University of Maine, Orono
Hellenic-American Union, Athens, Greece
Cedar Rapids Art Center, Iowa

1969 Harmon Galleries, Naples, FL
New Forms Gallery, Athens, Greece
Oehlschlaeger Galleries, Sarasota, FL

1970 Capricorn Galleries, Bethesda, MD

1971 Associated American Artists, NYC
ACA Galleries, NYC

1972 Garelick's Gallery, Detroit
Van Straaten Gallery, Chicago

1973 Capricorn Galleries, Bethesda, MD

1974 Oehlschlaeger Galleries, Sarasota, FL

1977 Syracuse University, Lowe Art Gallery,
     Syracuse, NY

1978 Oelschlaeger Galleries, Sarasota, FL

1979 Arwin Gallery, Detroit, MI

1980 Letterio Gallery, Chicago, IL
     Provincetown Group Gallery, MA
     Fine Arts Workshop, Provincetown, MA

1982 Pearce Museum, Chicago, IL

1985 Harmon-Meek Gallery, Naples, FL
     Midwest Museum of American Art,
     Elkhart, IN

1986 Canton Art Institute, Canton, OH
     Lakeview Museum of Arts, Peoria, IL

Selected Public Collections

Art Institute of Chicago
Art Museum, Tel Aviv, Israel
High Museum of Art, Atlanta, GA

Bibliotheque Nationale, Paris
Boymans Museum, Rotterdam, Netherlands
Butler Institute of American Art, Youngstown, OH

Cincinnati Art Museum
Columbia University, NY
Cornell University, Ithaca, NY

Dartmouth College, Hanover, NH
DePaul University, Chicago, IL
Detroit Institute of Arts

Gemeentemuseum, The Hague, Netherlands
Glasgow Art Gallery, Glasgow, Scotland

Hamburg Kunsthalle, Hamburg, Germany

Library of Congress, Washington, DC

Masillon Museum, Masillon, OH
Metropolitan Museum of Art, NYC
Montclair Museum, Montclair, NJ
Munson-Williams-Proctor Institute, Utica, NY
Museo d'Arte Moderne, Milan, Italy
Museo Nacional de Bellas Artes, Lima, Peru
Museu de Arte Moderne, Rio de Janeiro, Brazil
Museum am Ehrenhof, Dusseldorf, Germany

National Academy of Design, NYC
National Gallery of Art, Washington, DC
National Gallery of Art, Ottawa, Canada
National Museum, Stockholm, Sweden
New York Public Library
Ny Carlsberg Glypothek, Copenhagen, Denmark

Philadelphia Museum of Art
Provincetown Art Association

Smithsonian Institution, Washington, DC
Syracuse University

University of Chile, Santiago, Chile
University of Minnesota, Minneapolis

Van Gogh Foundation, Amsterdam, Netherlands
Victoria and Albert Museum, London, England

Worcester Art Museum, Worcester, MA

Yale University, New Haven, CT

Paris, 1963, color lithograph, 10¹/₄ x 7⁵/₈ inches

"Your environment comes in through your pores, through eyes, through all your senses and gets incorporated into a kind of general iconography, a kind of general storehouse or vocabulary of visual experience and visual information. . . .It's the sense, when living in Paris, of two thousand years of history, of all the people who have gone before me, of the smells of the streets, the quality of light . . . . Paris is a certain entity to me which is not only visual but it is comprised of people, food, the streets, the buildings. . ."

– *Richard Florsheim*

Richard Florsheim

Checklist of the Exhibition
(All measurements in inches)

PRINTS

1. *While Visions Weighed Him, Crushed and Speechless* (*War Portfolio*), 1940. Lithograph, 10 7/8 x 6 1/8. Courtesy of Richard Florsheim Art Fund.

2. *And Homeless Wandered* (*War Portfolio*), 1941. Lithograph, 9 11/16 x 12 5/16. Courtesy of Richard Florsheim Art Fund.

3. *Now Harbors Filled with Tangled Wreckage* (*War Portfolio*), 1945. Lithograph, 13 1/6 x 8 13/16. Courtesy of Richard Florsheim Art Fund.

4. *Insects* (*War Portfolio*), 1946. Lithograph, 5 1/8 x 7 7/16. Courtesy of Richard Florsheim Art Fund.

5. *The Land Once More Regains Its Cycle* (*War Portfolio*), 1946. Lithograph, 9 7/16 x 13 11/16. Courtesy of Richard Florsheim Art Fund.

6. *In Quest of Prophets* (*Each Man in His Time Portfolio*), 1951. Lithograph, 17 3/16 x 13 3/8. Courtesy of Richard Florsheim Art Fund.

7. *Inquisition,* 1953. Lithograph, 24 1/2 x 16 3/4. Courtesy of Richard Florsheim Art Fund.

8. *Crucifixion,* 1953. Lithograph, 26 15/16 x 17 3/4. Courtesy of Richard Florsheim Art Fund.

9. *Pines,* 1954. Color woodcut, 18 11/16 x 22 7/8. Courtesy of Syracuse University Art Collection.

10. *Pilings,* 1954. Color woodcut, 22 3/4 x 9 5/16. Courtesy of Richard Florsheim Art Fund.

11. *Bay,* 1955. Color woodcut, 7 x 22 7/8. Courtesy of Richard Florsheim Art Fund.

12. *Anchorage,* 1959. Lithograph, 13 7/8 x 9 7/8. Courtesy of Syracuse University Art Collection.

13. *Refinery,* 1961. Lithograph, 13 3/4 x 9 3/4. Courtesy of Richard Florsheim Art Fund.

14. *Shoreline,* 1962. Lithograph, 9 7/8 x 13 7/8. Courtesy of Richard Florsheim Art Fund.

15. *Skyscraper,* 1962. Color lithograph, 29 1/2 x 10 3/8. Courtesy of Richard Florsheim Art Fund.

16. *Paris,* 1963. Color lithograph, 10 1/4 x 7 5/8. Courtesy of Richard Florsheim Art Fund.

17. *Cathedral,* 1964. Lithograph, 17 9/16 x 13 15/16. Courtesy of Richard Florsheim Art Fund.

18. *Cathedral,* 1964. Color lithograph (yellow, red, and black), 17 9/16 x 13 15/16. Courtesy of Syracuse University Art Collection.

19. *Cathedral,* 1964. Color lithograph (blue, red and black), 17 9/16 x 13 15/16. Courtesy of Richard Florsheim Art Fund.

20. *Morning,* 1967. Color lithograph, 23 1/4 x 12 3/4. Courtesy of Richard Florsheim Art Fund.

21. *Morning,* 1967. Lithograph, 23 1/8 x 12 5/8. Courtesy of Richard Florsheim Art Fund.

22. *Combatants,* 1969. Color lithograph, 15 3/8 x 22 3/8. Courtesy of Richard Florsheim Art Fund.

23. *Dawn* (*Illuminations Portfolio*), 1970. Color lithograph, 13 9/16 x 18 1/8. Courtesy of Syracuse University Art Collection.

24. *Sun and Dunes* (*Illuminations Portfolio*), 1970. Color lithograph, 18 x 14. Courtesy of Richard Florsheim Art Fund.

25. *Luminescence* (*Illuminations Portfolio*), 1970. Color lithograph, 13 9/16 x 18 1/8. Courtesy of Syracuse University Art Collection.

26. *Factory Fires* (*Illuminations Portfolio*), 1970. Color lithograph, 18 x 14. Courtesy of Richard Florsheim Art Fund.

27. *Lightning* (*Illuminations Portfolio*), 1970. Color lithograph, 13 5/8 x 18. Courtesy of Richard Florsheim Art Fund.

28. *Fire* (*Illuminations Portfolio*), 1970. Color lithograph, 13 1/2 x 18 3/16. Courtesy of Richard Florsheim Art Fund.

29. *Bridge Lights* (*Illuminations Portfolio*), 1970. Color lithograph, 18 x 14. Courtesy of Richard Florsheim Art Fund.

30. *Blue Lights* (*Illuminations Portfolio*), 1970. Color lithograph, 18 x 14. Courtesy of Syracuse University Art Collection.

31. *Night Flight* (*Illuminations Portfolio*), 1970. Color lithograph, 13 1/2 x 18 1/16. Courtesy of Richard Florsheim Art Fund.

32. *Buoy* (*Illuminations Portfolio*), 1970.
Color lithograph, 18 1/4 x 14.
Courtesy of Richard Florsheim Art Fund.

33. *Neon Canyon* (*Illuminations Portfolio*), 1970.
Color lithograph, 18 1/16 x 14.
Courtesy of Richard Florsheim Art Fund.

34. *Night* (*Illuminations Portfolio*), 1970.
Color lithograph, 13 9/16 x 18 1/8.
Courtesy of Syracuse University Art Collection.

35. *Mooring*, 1970. Color lithograph, 14 x 10 1/16.
Courtesy of Richard Florsheim Art Fund.

36. *Crowd*, 1970. Color lithograph, 15 3/4 x 22 1/8.
Courtesy of Richard Florsheim Art Fund.

37. *Fireworks*, 1972. Color lithograph, 29 15/16 x 18.
Courtesy of Richard Florsheim Art Fund.

38. *Neon Night*, 1972.
Color lithograph, 22 13/16 x 17 3/8.
Courtesy of Richard Florsheim Art Fund.

39. *Spinning Machine*, 1972.
Color lithograph, 12 1/8 x 24.
Courtesy of Richard Florsheim Art Fund.

40. *Variations on a Seashore*, 1973.
Lithograph, 22 7/8 x 15 3/4.
Courtesy of Richard Florsheim Art Fund.

41. *Catalysts*, 1978.
Color lithograph, 9 x 12.
Courtesy of Richard Florsheim Art Fund.

42. *Silhouette*, 1979.
Lithograph, 20 x 8.
Courtesy of Richard Florsheim Art Fund.

PAINTINGS

43. *Poles in Landscape*, 1936.
Egg tempera on paper board, 14 1/2 x 21 1/4.
Courtesy of Richard Florsheim Art Fund.

44. *Attack*, 1940.
Egg tempera on gesso board, 20 x 20.
Courtesy of Richard Florsheim Art Fund.

45. *#3 (War Scenes) Untitled*, c. 1940-45.
Casein on board, 18 1/2 x 13 3/4.
Courtesy of Richard Florsheim Art Fund.

46. *#5 (War Scenes) Chain and the Man*, c. 1940-45.
Casein on board, 14 1/2 x 21.
Courtesy of Richard Florsheim Art Fund.

47. *Sajuaros*, 1946.
Oil on gesso panel, 11 x 10.
Courtesy of Richard Florsheim Art Fund.

48. *Survival*, 1946. Oil on canvas, 14 x 26.
Courtesy of Richard Florsheim Art Fund.

49. *Men and Crosses*, 1949.
Oil on canvas, 14 x 15.
Courtesy of Richard Florsheim Art Fund.

50. *The Passage of Time*, 1949-50.
Oil on canvas, 24 x 32.
Courtesy of Harmon-Meek Gallery, Naples, Florida.

51. *Cockfight*, 1950.
Oil on canvas, 24 x 32.
Courtesy of Richard Florsheim Art Fund.

52. *Mexican Walls*, 1951.
Oil on canvas, 36 x 20.
Courtesy of Richard Florsheim Art Fund.

53. *Skull*, 1952.
Oil on canvas, 40 x 30.
Courtesy of Richard Florsheim Art Fund.

54. *Monument to Monuments*, 1954.
Oil on canvas, 72 x 24.
Courtesy of Richard Florsheim Art Fund.

55. *Earth Fire*, 1970.
Oil on canvas, 18 x 24.
Collection of
Drs. Paul and Laura Mesaros, Steubenville, Ohio.

56. *Night City IV*, 1970.
Wax & oil on board, 18 x 12.
Collection of R. M. Pine, Elmhurst, Illinois.

57. *Celebration*, 1976.
Oil on canvas, 36 x 24.
Collection of
Dr. and Mrs. August L. Freundlich, Lutz, Florida.

58. *Crucible*, 1970s.
Oil on canvas, 30 x 40.
Courtesy of Richard Florsheim Art Fund.

59. *Cathedral*, 1970s.
Oil on gesso panel, 36 x 12.
Courtesy of Richard Florsheim Art Fund.

" I believe that man is essentially good. Given freedom of
... spirit and thought, he will behave with dignity and understanding towards his fellow. He will be the creator, not the destroyer.
Only when he is afraid is he cruel and hateful. When he undersands
and has insight, the Golden Rule does not have to be imposed on
him from without; it comes from the depth of his nature."

– Richard Florsheim

©Norma Holt